SOMETHING SURE SMELLS AROUND HERE

LIMERICKS

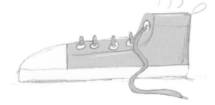

BRIAN P. CLEARY

ILLUSTRATIONS BY
ANDY ROWLAND

M MILLBROOK PRESS/MINNEAPOLIS

To my little
Stinky . . . Alice
—AR

To the
Norman kids
—BPC

Millbrook Press
A division of Lerner Publishing Group, Inc.
241 First Avenue North
Minneapolis, MN 55401 USA

For reading levels and more information, look up this title at www.lernerbooks.com.

Main body text set in Klepto ITC Std Regular 15/27.
Typeface provided by International Typeface Corp.

Library of Congress Cataloging-in-Publication Data

Cleary, Brian P., 1959– author.
    Something sure smells around here: Limericks / by Brian P. Cleary ; illustrated by Andy Rowland
        pages   cm. — (Poetry Adventures)
    ISBN 978-1-4677-2044-1 (lib. bdg. : alk. paper)
    ISBN 978-1-4677-6035-5 (pbk.)
    ISBN 978-1-4677-6302-8 (EB pdf)
    1. Limericks, Juvenile. 2. Poetry—Authorship. I. Rowland, Andrew, 1962– illustrator. II. Title.
PN6231.L5C58 2015
808.1'75—dc23   2014009380

Manufactured in the United States of America
1 – DP – 12/31/14

TABLE OF CONTENTS

What Is a Limerick?

Limericks are fun to read and even more fun to write! They are a short, rhyming, and nearly always funny form of poetry that tell a story, and they have a few simple rules.

Limericks are five lines long. There is a rhythm—almost a musical beat—to these poems. The first, second, and fifth lines rhyme with one another. The length of lines 1, 2, and 5 may vary, but they each are generally between eight and ten syllables or beats.

The first two lines often introduce the subject of the poem.

On airplanes, my friend Janey Dobbin
would sweat and her head would start throbbin'.

The third and fourth rhyme with each other, but not with lines 1, 2, and 5. They are also shorter in length—usually five to six syllables.

Each time she would go up,
she'd say as she'd throw up,

The last line wraps up the poem. Remember, you're telling a story, so even though this is short, your verse still has a beginning, a middle, and an end.

Some people even come up with the last line first and then try to write the rest of the poem around it.

"It's a good thing that I'm not a robin."

When you start writing your own limericks, remember these few rules, plus the most important one: have fun!

There once was a student named Sonny

who bought books of jokes with his money.

He ate one at lunchtime,

then gave as his punch line,

"That tasted a little bit funny."

A frog drove her car down the road.

Hearing one of her tires explode,

the frog didn't panic—

she called her mechanic,

and next thing you know, she was *toad*.

One evening, a boy named Carmelo

dreamed he ate an enormous marshmallow.

He woke up at dawn,

and his pillow was gone.

When he screamed, he saw feathers, poor fellow.

Fun-loving Steve is quite spunky.

He's out every night getting funky.

Tonight he's at Anna's

with a bunch of bananas.

Did I mention that Steve is a monkey?

My laptop, with skill and finesse,

has a brain that can beat me at chess.

But with no arms or body,

it stinks at karate.

Now please help me clean up this mess.

A teacher of English, Ms. White,

whose students got everything right,

would put on her shades

as she wrote down her grades

because all of her kids were so bright.

Early one Mother's Day, Jake
decided that he'd like to bake
a pie for his mother,
but soon he'd discover
it surely was no piece of cake.

An eye whispered once to an ear,

with a hint of disdain and a sneer.

As its eyebrow arose,

it glanced down at the nose

and said, "Something sure smells around here."

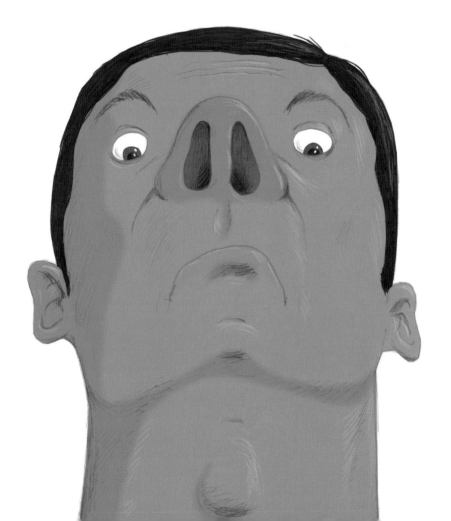

Said clockmaker Hans Gerdenhopp,

as he suddenly came to a stop,

"You can't understand

a clock with one hand.

I must go to a secondhand shop."

"Ahoy!" said a pirate named MARRRRty,

who was fun loving, healthy, and heARRRRRty.

"I believe it's my duty

to go shake my booty,

'cause nothin's more fun than a pARRRRty!"

Said little first-grader Pam Plunkett,

"The past tense of 'shrink it' is 'shrunk it.'"

Told, "Yes, that is true!

Just who taught that to you?"

she said, "Not really sure, I just thunk it."

On the acres of Old Farmer Akkers,

you'll find there's no hay, no wheat stackers,

no pigpens, no plows—

only ducklings and cows.

He calls his place "Just Milk and Quackers."

Our little Welsh corgi named Bramley

does not like our mailman, Stanley.

He'll tear 'cross the floor,

bark and leap at the door,

and then act like he's just saved our family.

I met a young spider named Deb,

who's become quite a singing celeb.

When I asked how she'd grown

to be so well known,

she replied, "I'm all over the web!"

A French chef we all call Miss Margot

cooks lunch at our school here in Fargo.

But we wouldn't eat

any yucky frog meat,

so she makes somethin' she calls "S cargo."

A great pasta maker named Freddy

cooked eight hundred pounds of spaghetti.

He carted it down

to the center of town,

rang a bell, and then yelled, "Supper's ready!"

Our neighbor is nice Mrs. Rands.

She forgets names and faces and plans.

She has such amnesia

that each time she sees ya,

she tells you her name and shakes hands.

A talented student named Haley

could play the French horn, ukulele,

the oboe, viola,

the drums, and mandola.

Her neighbors could vouch for that . . . daily.

Mom said our dog's part retriever,

part collie, part badger and beaver,

and part German shepherd,

part penguin, part leopard.

I'm not sure if I should believe her.

A man on a bus in Manhattan

was fluent in German and Latin.

Though he could speak either,

we found he used neither

when he looked down and saw what he sat in.

I once met an artist named Hank.

To put it quite bluntly, he stank.

Couldn't paint, couldn't sketch,

and it wasn't a stretch

to say he could not draw a blank.

Our new teacher's name is Ms. Lester.

Before her we had Mrs. Chester,

Mrs. Brown, Mr. Lee,

Mrs. O'Rafferty. . . .

Can we scare off one more this semester?

Biking, Mackenzie once rode

down a street—heard a "pop"—and she slowed.

In discovering that

her front tire was flat,

she said, "Must be that fork in the road!"

A short, gutsy kid from Milwaukee
tried football and rugby and hockey.
He was cut from those teams
but adjusted his dreams
and today is a prosperous jockey.

A cat who spoke only chimpanzee

thought, "No master I've had understands me.

I just *eee-eee-ah-oohed*

for my kitty cat food,

but bananas are all that he hands me."

A limerick poet, Ms. Sheets,

starts poems she never completes . . .

The End

FURTHER READING

BOOKS

Brooks, Lou. *Twimericks: The Book of Tongue-Twisting Limericks.* New York: Workman, 2009. Challenge yourself to say these "twimericks"— limerick tongue twisters!

Cleary, Brian P. *Rainbow Soup: Adventures in Poetry.* Minneapolis: Millbrook Press, 2004. Discover poems of all kinds in this entertaining collection.

Macken, Joanne Early. *Read, Recite, and Write Limericks.* New York: Crabtree, 2014. Learn tricks with word sounds and repetition that can help you create fun rhymes.

WEBSITES

Giggle Poetry: How to Write a Limerick
http://www.gigglepoetry.com /poetryclassdetail.aspx?LessonPlanID=2
Get more tips about writing your own limericks.

Kenn Nesbitt's Poetry for Kids
http://www.poetry4kids.com
The website of children's poet Kenn Nesbitt is full of funny poems, games, contests, videos, and more.

Limerick Factory
http://www.learner.org/teacherslab/math/patterns /limerick/limerick_acttxt.html
Make your own limerick by choosing phrases from an online template.